Vertical Gardening: More Garden in Less Space

Gardening Basics for Beginners Series

Nina Greene

This book is dedicated to all aspiring green thumbs.

Copyright © 2014 by Speedy Publishing LLC

All rights reserved. No part of this publication may be reproduced, distributed or transmitted in any form or by any means, including photocopying, recording, or other electronic or mechanical methods, without the prior written permission of the publisher, except in the case of brief quotations embodied in critical reviews and certain other noncommercial uses permitted by copyright law. For permission requests, write to the publisher, addressed "Attention: Permissions Coordinator," at the address below.

Speedy Publishing LLC (c) 2014
40 E. Main St., #1156
Newark, DE 19711
www.speedypublishing.co

Ordering Information:

Quantity sales; Special discounts are available on quantity purchases by corporations, associations, and others. For details, contact the "Special Sales Department" at the address above.

-- 1st edition

Manufactured in the United States of America

Table of Contents

Publisher's Notes i

Chapter 1: Introduction to Vertical Gardens 1

Chapter 2: Vertical Gardening – What is It? 3

Chapter 3: Vertical Garden Design 7

Chapter 4: Choosing and Preparing the Right Spot For Your Vertical Garden 11

Chapter 5: Arbors, Arches, and Trellises 18

Chapter 6: Containers and Hanging Planters 26

Chapter 7: Living Walls 30

Chapter 8: Choosing Fruits and Vegetables 34

Chapter 9: Weeds, Fertilizing, and Pruning 36

Chapter 10: Controlling Pests 40

Chapter 11: Conclusion 44

Meet the Author.................................. 46

More Books by Nina Greene 48

PUBLISHER'S NOTES

Disclaimer

This publication is intended to provide helpful and informative material. It is not intended to diagnose, treat, cure, or prevent any health problem or condition, nor is intended to replace the advice of a physician. No action should be taken solely on the contents of this book. Always consult your physician or qualified health-care professional on any matters regarding your health and before adopting any suggestions in this book or drawing inferences from it.

The author and publisher specifically disclaim all responsibility for any liability, loss or risk, personal or otherwise, which is incurred as a consequence, directly or indirectly, from the use or application of any contents of this book.

Any and all product names referenced within this book are the trademarks of their respective owners. None of these owners have sponsored, authorized, endorsed, or approved this book.

Always read all information provided by the manufacturers' product labels before using their products. The author and publisher are not responsible for claims made by manufacturers.

Print Edition 2014

Chapter 1: Introduction to Vertical Gardens

Vertical gardens allow gardens to grow in very small spaces, as well as in places like cities where land is not available. Vertical gardening reduces the area occupied by plants because they grow upwards and off of the ground. Your fruits and vegetables are protected from damage because they are not in contact with the earth which reduces the use of pesticides. And vertical gardening also makes harvesting the rewards of your

1

labor much easier than traditional methods.

Whether you are new to gardening or just new to vertical gardening, this book is designed to provide you with the basic knowledge you need to grow a vibrant and abundant vertical garden.

Chapter 2: Vertical Gardening – What is It?

Vertical gardening is a method that trains plants to grow upward and off the ground rather than spreading out on the ground surface. Conventional gardening methods use up a lot of land and are not possible in densely populated urban areas. Vertical gardening is a great way to maximize the use of land, to grow a garden in very tight areas, or maintain a garden in places where no actual land is available such as balconies. You can literally grow anything you choose, as long as you have the right knowledge and the space for it.

Vertical gardening makes the practice of growing your own fruits, vegetables, herbs and other plants an equal opportunity sport. Vertical gardening cuts down on the traditional labor, time and space needed to grow food or keep a blah space beautiful. It reduces the amount of pests, pesticides, or other soil and mold-born contaminants that are common in standard gardening methods.

Vertical gardening is not new. Some of the first known vertical gardens were The Hanging Gardens of Babylon in 600 BC which are considered one of the Seven Wonders of the World. (With new evidence, there is some argument over whether the gardens were actually in Babylon, but they did exist.) If you travel, you can see multiple examples of the beauty and architecture of green walls and architecture.

It's possible to have a very large garden in a limited space. Almost anything can be grown vertically. Herbs, flowers, vegetables and some fruits are options for:

- Apartment dwellers
- Gardeners with small yards
- Conventional gardeners who have run out of ground space
- Schools and retirement communities
- Gardeners who live in especially pest-prone areas

- Gardeners who want to cut down on labor
- People who want to reduce the use of pesticides and eat more organically grown fruits and vegetables
- Gardeners who need to produce higher yields in less space
- People who hate pulling weeds
- Everyone who enjoys more flavorful fruits and vegetables

Chapter 3: Vertical Garden Design

The design possibilities for a vertical garden are only limited by one's surroundings, imagination or budget. Designing a vertical garden requires good planning. Don't feel limited. Magazine-ready trellises may be the most dreamed of designs, but the options are numerous. Structural supports can be imaginative, beautiful and functional.

Structures should minimizing maintenance. They can be strictly functional, purely aesthetic, or both. It's up to you!

Three common vertical garden designs to choose from are:

Do It Yourself (DIY) – these designs utilize common household items such as gutters, fencing, pots, walls, and balconies.

Kits - Kits implement the use of ready to construct benches, planters, trellises, arches, arbors, frames, towers, etc.

Professional Design – a professionally designed garden is created and installed by a paid landscaper or garden artist; most commonly used for large projects and commercial/public areas.

Regardless of the design method chosen, vertical gardens have some limitations. Be sure to take location, plant type, structures and watering into consideration during the planning process.

Your vertical garden will require ample sunlight and plenty of water. Be sure that trees, structures or other items do not shade your vertical garden, and make sure that water is accessible through a hose.

When using walls or structures in your vertical garden, it is important to consider weight (including the weight of your plants, what you're growing, and the degree to which they need to be trained to grow vertically.) Soil can be very heavy, especially when damp. Walls and structures need to be capable of withstanding the weight of multiple plants, planters, baskets, etc. The use of cinder blocks is a creative way to grow multiple plants. They also provide for some clever design options!

CHAPTER 4: CHOOSING AND PREPARING THE RIGHT SPOT FOR YOUR VERTICAL GARDEN

Your first task should be identifying a good location for your garden. Growing vertically allows you 6 cubic feet of growing space for every square foot of growing space available. A vertical garden can be placed virtually anywhere but its location has a direct impact on your garden's growth and development. Not every space provides the best environment for growing plants vertically. An ideal location will have good exposure to sunlight.

Choosing Your Plants

Vertical gardening is not limited to just growing vegetables; it can also be used to propagate decorative plants. Choosing what to grow is important – most, but not all plants can be trained to grow upwards. Some plants are genetically more grounded to the earth and may require a different type of structure. In the case of more stubborn plants, a structure that will support multiple pots will be necessary. Each plant carries different requirements. Tomatoes grow best in wire cages, but their tendrils allow for some experimentation with placement. Twining vegetables like peas and long beans naturally grow upward and will need trellises, long poles, or fences in order to thrive. If your experience goes well, you can experiment with chicken wire, arches, arbors, and towers.

If space is at a real premium, you'll want to avoid vine-heavy plants like pumpkins, cucumbers, and squash. Weigh your options aesthetically as well. Because some plants do produce more foliage than others, consider how much green you want to see as well as manage. Even in the tiniest drab settings, there's no reason why your garden can't provide a little spot of life and color!

Some plants grow well together. With a bit of investigation you can find out what plants grow quickly and get along together in tight spaces. Radishes, cabbage, spinach and lettuce can provide a quick, ready supply of vegetables under a canopy of vines.

Preparing the Soil

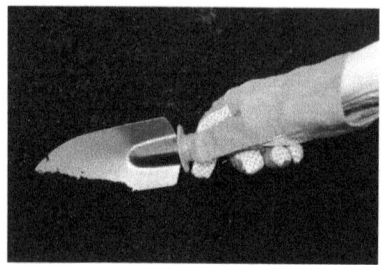

After you have chosen your desired plants, it is time to prepare and cultivate the soil. The quality of soil is crucial for plant growth in any garden. This will require weeding out grass and other plants in the area and tilling the soil. If the existing dirt is not rich enough to support a garden, the addition of compost-rich soil may be necessary. In cases where there is no actual land to till, like a vertical garden on a balcony or patio, the pots or containers that are going to be used should also include good garden soil.

Planting Your Garden

After choosing and preparing the location for your vertical garden, you are finally ready to start planting. You can start with seeds or seedlings, but if you're starting later in the spring, use seedlings. If you're very (very) new to gardening, start with an herb, like mint, or some chilies, or lettuce. When planting a naturally climbing plant, the structures it will cling onto can be constructed later after the plant has grown sufficiently in size. However, in the case of earth-bound plants, your structures need to be constructed first- you need them to support and hold your pots and containers.

Pots and Containers

If you choose to grow plants in containers, you need to select the right ones you're your plants. All containers should be deep enough to accommodate the plants and their roots as they grow. Any signs of discoloration in the plant or the container are an indication that the container needs to be swapped out. Remember that larger and heavier plants require bigger and stronger containers to support them as they grow. Regardless of a container's size, be sure each one has drainage holes in the bottom before filling them with soil.

When choosing baskets, be sure to use a heavier weight basket that shows no signs of previous use, drying out, or that shows signs of pest infestation. The basket should be deep enough to allow two inches of clearance from topsoil to the basket's edge.

Chapter 5: Arbors, Arches, and Trellises

Arbors, arches, and trellises add a distinctive touch to a vertical garden. These popular structures have aesthetic appeal but also serve a variety of functions. A vertical garden structure will help your plants grow up rather than out.

Arbors – these are usually located in entryways, and many people use them to plant greenery as demarcation and decoration for gates. They have roof elements that serve as a climbing structure for vines and flowering plants such as ivy, Betty Corning clematis and Dortmund roses. Some arbors are made large enough to cover walkways, and they provide shade. Some arbors use designs made to look like an extension of the home.

An arbor doesn't have to require construction. Plant trees to create a truly natural structure. Choose fruit trees that are native to your area and add another crop to your garden.

Arches - arches may or may not have roof elements. Arches can be used to create a focal point in a garden area. They are used as a garden accent to showcase beautiful flowering vines and plants like passion flowers and jasmine.

Trellises – trellises are stand-alone pieces that work as a climbing path for vines and other plants that are trained to grow upward such as bougainvillea, trumpet vine and wisteria. They can disguise unsightly areas of a garden-a blank wall of a barn, a worn shed, a garage or other section of your house.

Taking some heavy twine and attaching it to your fence or structure in a zigzag pattern, or simply straight up or straight down can create an inexpensive trellis.

Well-constructed and well-placed garden trellises increase the leaf-to-fruit (or vegetable or herb) ratio of the plant by allowing more leaves access to sun. A good support will allow you to see and reach through the vines to harvest your crop; it must be strong and stable enough to hold the plants it's supporting.

Research what you most want to grow before you start building for best results. For example, peas (all varieties) may grow anywhere from 2 to 6 feet, and the pods of some varieties are heavier than others. Rye may need extra space, depending on what's being planted beside it.

Only build trellises and supports that you can safely reach. Don't let ambition or a lack of knowledge lead to injury.

Other Materials That Can be used as Supports

Depending on your surroundings and creativity, other structures and items can be used or incorporated into a vertical garden. For example, unsightly walls and fencing (wood or chain-link) can be covered with climbing plants, flowers, and vegetables such as blematis, climbing hydrangea, various honeysuckles, climbing roses, morning glories, tiger lilies, cucumbers and tomatoes. Fence posts can also be used as the support for the bean members of the vegetable family. (Be sure to attach the primary stem to the post for greater stability.)

When purchasing supportive structures, consider what parts of your garden that you plan to rotate. What you rotate and how often will influence the strength (bamboo poles or t-stakes for temporary plantings, for example, or the use of wire, over choosing a permanent in-ground installation).

Examples of temporary supports you can create for heavy rotation crops:

Loop cotton or jute lines (or any other strong plant-based or biodegradable material to use for ties-especially for heavier plants or those that need extra help growing vertically) around standing stakes or posts. If you use biodegradable materials as temporary supports, then it's easy to take down a trellis, arbor, etc., and pull out the plants there on the spot. Then, what you no longer use can be added to the compost pile, helping you keep a regular supply of gardening soil while saving money at the same time.

The most successful garden trellises increase the leaf-to-fruit ratio of the plant by allowing more leaves access to sun. A good support should also allow you to see and reach through the vines to harvest your crop, and it must be strong enough to hold its load.

A well-placed support structure should face north to accommodate particularly sun-hungry plants. Be aware that this is not always the case. Vegetables and fruits that prefer shade are the same ones you usually see in the ground, like arugula, celery, collard greens, Swiss chard, potatoes, cucumbers, rhubarb, and kale, to name a few.

Most herbs will also require some shade. Be especially mindful of basil, mint, oregano, chives, and parsley.

Of course, there are degrees of shade, and shade requirements vary from plant to plant. If you're feeling unsure about what to plant and where, visit your nearest gardening store, or ask some good friends who garden.

Chapter 6: Containers and Hanging Planters

There are numerous vertical gardening containers and hanging planters that can be used and are often already in your home.

Some of the most popular vertical gardening containers and hanging planters you can use, and they are often already in your home.

Gutters - Gutters are the most fund-friendly technique for creating a vertical garden. (They're also durable!)

Purchase inexpensive plastic gutters or repurpose old gutters. Simply drill drainage holes in the bottom, fill them with soil and start planting. Gardeners can choose simple straight columns or aim for a more complex arrangement.

Hanging Planters - Hanging planters can be bought or made depending on needs and the desired aesthetic effect. Some of the most common items that can be turned into hanging planters are large bottles and cans.

Shoe Organizers – Canvas or vinyl hanging shoe organizers (holders) are generally used for small plant types due to their size. Shoe organizers are capable of holding large quantities of water, so you can schedule watering less often.

Stacked Pots - Stacked pots are not directly installed on a wall. They are typically placed on the ground. The pots are "stacked" together in such a way that it provides room for five or more plants. This is ideal for flower growers- the stacking system allows for multiple blooms. You can apply as much color as you like!

Other options to try:

A-frames
Pergolas
Raised beds
Barrels
Netting
Topsy-Turvy planters

The possibilities for designing a vertical garden are numerous. If you're looking for inspiration, check out blogs and online forums for more ideas and helpful tips.

CHAPTER 7: LIVING WALLS

A wall is all it takes to launch your very first vertical garden project. Usually called a green wall, this type of vertical garden is classified into two styles: living walls and green facades.

Green facades are often the product of traditional vine gardening. It uses typical garden planters and supports, soil, and is commonly constructed on exterior walls. Climbing plants either grow directly on the ground or in customized planters built as part of the building or structure. Most green facades are focused on vegetable or home gardening. Ivy-covered houses in Germany, called grünes haus, are testimonies to their aesthetic potential.

The French botanist and artist Patrick Blanc pioneered the first vertical garden over 30 years ago. Living walls have recently gained popularity, in urban areas. They exhibit a more convenient gardening system than green facades. Many incorporate irrigation instruments and have versatile designs.

In creating living walls, there are three options:

    Loose
    Mat
    Structure

A wall "loosely" created uses soil that is placed in a container or bag and is then attached to the wall. This setup is ideal for creating garden displays outdoors, but it can be messy indoors. The soil will also need to be replenished periodically over time.

Mat systems are the most available non-soil system on the market for the creation of vertical gardening. They are popular in hydroponic gardening, where special fabrics act as a replacement for soil. Mat systems offer pocket-like planters that focus on water conservation and air circulation. They are readily installed on dry walls or are placed on hooks. Some companies provide different varieties of climbing plants, fertilizers, and even watering kits with timers to help optimize your indoor garden.

A structural medium is the easiest to maintain but is the most expensive to install. They are made of blocks that can be customized for specific wall designs, plant variety, or watering specifications.

Make sure that your walls have been properly waterproofed before installation. You will need to decide whether to water the plants green wall yourself or whether to install an irrigation system (which is usually part of the pricier structural setup). It all depends on the extent of your wall garden and of course, your budget.

As with an outdoor garden, there are few limits as to what you can grow. With some research and creativity, you can easily bring the outdoors indoors.

Chapter 8: Choosing Fruits and Vegetables

Growing fruits and vegetables in a vertical garden is a great way to cultivate more food in less space. Growing your own fresh fruits and veggies saves time and money. Crops are less likely to acquire soil-borne diseases. Fungus and rotten food is also eliminated because crops are off the ground, allowing for better air circulation. Growing your own food in a vertical garden is also healthier for you and your family because the need for pesticides is nearly non-existent.

Ideal crops to grow are vine types rather than bush types. However, most vine type plants do not naturally grab hold of a fence or a wall and climb vertically. The primary stem needs to be threaded around and through a fence, pickets, trellis, wall, or post to train it to grow upwards.

Chapter 9: Weeds, Fertilizing, and Pruning

Like horizontal gardening, vertical plants need proper maintenance for healthy growth. If you are thinking of starting a living wall but fear that weeds, fertilization and pruning might be complicated, this is not the case.

Weeds

Removal of weeds for vertical gardens should be taken care of as often as possible. Keep in mind that the limited space means that plants cannot afford to have competition in their area. Weeds should be taken out the minute they are spotted.

Fertilization

Fertilization is a must in vertical gardens and especially for vegetable plants. Properly fertilized plants will be healthy without any trace of insects or diseases. Fertilizer needs to be mixed into the soil prior to planting and then added as needed on a routine basis. It is important to water and check your plants; soil regularly to prevent the soil from drying out.

Pruning

The pruning process for vertical gardens is basically the same as it is for horizontal gardens. The only difference is that the gardener needs to be stricter with plants limitations due to the small amount of space. Vertical pruning is plant-specific. This means gardeners need to find out exactly what type of plant they are growing and learn how to prune it properly. For example, those who are growing vertical tomatoes need to prune the blossoms before the plant matures to ensure the best results.

Weeding, fertilization and pruning will vary slightly depending on the vertical garden style selected. A garden composed of stacked pots or hanging planters will have different maintenance requirements then plants that climb walls and structures or plants that need to be tied back to stakes or trellises.

Beginners should start with a small batch of the same type plants before adding variety.

Chapter 10: Controlling Pests

Vertical gardens have fewer pests and are seldom attacked by rodents. Diseases are not as destructive in vertical gardens due to increased air circulation with flowers, vines and crops up off the ground.

Spotting potential insect infestations and removing them is far easier. Fruits and vegetables are cleaner, have fewer deformities and are less susceptible to rot. Pest problems can arise from factors such as the crops or plants grown, their location and/or the items or structures that are used in a vertical garden.

Climbing plants that are rooted in soil are apt to require more preventive pest care and maintenance then plants in a vertical garden. Become informed on the different kinds of pests most likely to seek out the plants in your garden so you know what to look for. If you find plants infested with unwanted critters, immediately take action to prevent pests from spreading to other plants or parts of your garden.

Before using pesticides, try blasting bugs off your plants with strong bursts of water. Rub the plant stems with a cloth to destroy dormant insect eggs. If pesticides cannot be avoided, organic and biologically safe products are recommended. Here are a few suggestions that you can find in your own kitchen:

Garlic and/or onions – great for killing soft bodied insects. Direct sprays can paralyze flying insects. Also works as a fungicide. These work best if crushed or liquefied in a vegetable oil tea. Use several cloves of garlic per gallon of water.

Hot Peppers – fresh or powder is great for repelling rabbits and other pests. Pepper's acidic "burning" effect will take care of most soft bodied insects. Best when mixed with garlic spray applications.

Canola oil, vegetable oils – oil sprays suffocate soft bodied insects. Don't use too much on sensitive plants. (These oils may burn leaves.) Don't use no more than 1 cup of oil per gallon of water.

Note that mineral oils also work, but they are made from petroleum products.

Chapter 11: Conclusion

Vertical Gardening virtually eliminates all objections and excuses for not growing a garden in a limited space. Whether you would like to have a garden for cultivating herbs, fruits and vegetables, or simply for style, a beginning gardener can be successful growing up instead of out. Vertical gardens can beautify your space with hanging baskets, twining vines, climbing roses, or provide inexpensive fresh fruits and veggies for your family. Vertical gardens are practical and create an aesthetic appeal as they grow and thrive.

MEET THE AUTHOR

Nina Greene grew up a country kid in the foothills of Northern California and acquired her love for the outdoors, gardening and landscaping from her father.

Forty-plus years later, Nina still resides in Nor Cal and tends to her organic garden that provides fresh fruit, vegetables and herbs for family, friends, neighbors, co-workers and occasional wildlife.

Nina's *Gardening Basics for Beginners Series* is designed to help future garden enthusiasts get their hands dirty without feeling overwhelmed from information overload.

More Books by Nina Greene

Gardening Basics for Beginners.

Garden Styles: Introduction to 25 Garden Styles

www.ingramcontent.com/pod-product-compliance
Ingram Content Group UK Ltd.
Pitfield, Milton Keynes, MK11 3LW, UK
UKHW022120230426
12048UKWH00010BA/619